GW01564182

Reinhold Messner

The Goddess of Turquoise

The Way to Cho Oyu

Reinhold Messner

The Goddess of Turquoise

The Way to Cho Oyu

Introduction, bibliography and notes by

Fosco Maraini

Illustrations by

Kapa Gyalzen and Pasang Norbu

Translated from the German by
Philip Pierce

PILGRIMS PUBLISHING
◆ Varanasi ◆

Picture opposite: A typical Khampa.

The Goddess of Turquoise: The Way to Cho Oyu
Reinhold Messner

Translated from the German by Philip Pierce

Published by:
PILGRIMS PUBLISHING

An imprint of:
PILGRIMS BOOK HOUSE
(Distributors in India)
B 27/98 A-8, Nawabganj Road
Durga Kund, Varanasi-221010, India
Tel: 91-542-2314059, 2314060, 2312456
E-mail: pilgrims@satyam.net.in
Website: www.pilgrimsbooks.com

PILGRIMS BOOK HOUSE (New Delhi)
9 Netaji Subhash Marg, 2nd Floor
Near Neeru Hotel, Daryaganj, New Delhi 110002
Tel: 91-11-23285081
E-mail: pilgrim@del2.vsnl.net.in

Distributed in Nepal by:
PILGRIMS BOOK HOUSE
P O Box 3872, Thamel,
Kathmandu, Nepal
Tel: 977-1-4700942, Off: 977-1-4700919, Fax: 977-1-4700943
E-mail: pilgrims@wlink.com.np

First English Edition Copyright © 2005, Pilgrims Publishing
All Rights Reserved

Edited by Christopher N Burchett
Layout by Asha Mishra
Picture credits: All photos in the text by Reinhold Messner.

ISBN: 81-7769-213-5

The contents of this book may not be reproduced, stored or copied in any form—printed, electronic, photocopied, or otherwise—except for excerpts used in review, without the written permission of the publisher.

Printed in India at Pilgrim Press Pvt. Ltd. Lalpur, Varanasi

The Migration of the Sherpas

Call up your powers of imagination; an entire people on the move from one place of settlement to another, perhaps very far away. This is one of the most extraordinary kinds of drama in the history of mankind. The great migration that set the pattern for the exodus from Egypt that led Moses and his people into the land of Canaan comes immediately to mind. This event is famous, though, because great poets described it, and because their account entered into the holiest books of the Western canon. How many other migrations, perhaps equally as dramatic and involving equally as much suffering, have succumbed to oblivion? How many others have only fragmentarily been retained in human memory?

Many years ago, in 1968, I had the opportunity to make several trips into the mountains of Friuli. A friend showed me the valleys through which, 1,400 years earlier, in April 568, the Lombards are presumed to have swooped down into Italy. Sitting on a boulder, I studied the serene valley floor with its asphalt road. Every now and then there was movement; a delivery truck, a freight train. The peaceful hum of the daily traffic reached up into the heights. I took a moment's pleasure in closing my eyes and returning in my fantasy, to April of the year 568. Did the sun shine during those days? Did it rain? No one knows. Certainly the way was a bumpy one, muddy or dusty depending on the weather. Over it came the vanguard of the new barbarians, proud, martial men astride horses, heavily armed, ready to put any opponent to flight. Then others, and still others, for hours on end. There followed the majestic specimens of horses belonging to King Alboin and his court. Many hours later, perhaps only the next day, appeared the masses of commoners; wagons with women, children and the elderly, accompanied by herds driven forward with calls, yells and whistles, and trailed by barking dogs. The poor cows wished

Sherpa in Solu-Khumbu.

to graze, but no, it was ever onward. And then once more came groups of armed men who protected the flanks, and finally a huge armed force that covered the rear and closed out the prodigious column.

It is estimated that the number of Lombards was over two hundred thousand. They had left their homeland in Noricum and Pannonia in order to escape from under the pressure of the Gepidae and other enemies, and confidently headed towards the fabled plains of Italy, a fertile and sunny land, a land of vineyards and gardens, cities and citadels. And the Romans? They had once been the rulers of the world, but by now the barbarians knew all too well that they no longer mattered.

King Liutprand (712-744) flew into a rage when the Byzantines cited a Roman: A Romane! dicamus, hoc solo nomine quidquid ignobilitatis, quidquid timiditatis, quidquid avaritiae, quidquid luxuriae, quidquid mendacii, imo quidquid vitiorum est comprehendente[1].

As for the Eastern Empire, it was too remote to cause any trepidation. The risks involved in hazarding the venture, advancing boldly, occupying fertile territory and seizing the cities with their forums, markets, theatres and baths, and their basilicas rich in gold and marble, would be worth it. The undertaking, which may have seemed unpromising to many, was completely successful. A few years later, in 572, Alboin and his court were residing in royal splendour in Pavia, and for two hundred years Italy was called the land of the Lombards.

One of the least known, and at the same time one of the boldest, of the many migrations woven throughout human history, is the

---

[1]Quoted from Carlo Tagliavini, **Le orgini delle lingue neolatine**, 5th ed. (Bologna: Patron, 1969), 163.

6

A scene in Khami Manu on a Tibetan pony.
The woman is riding on a yak.

one that led a small, courageous group of Tibetans from the valleys in the region of Kham, in the extreme eastern part of old Tibet near the border of the Chinese province of Szechwan, to certain valleys of the Himalaya. They ended their journey at the foot of lofty mountains, the most vertiginous heights on earth; Chomolungma (Mount Everest) and other colossi among its retinue.

Unfortunately no bard sang the memorable deeds of these Tibetans, who one day left tented camps and pastures, houses and villages, and set off into the unknown. All of this was long shrouded in darkest mystery. It was only in recent years that a German scholar, Michael Oppitz of the University of Cologne, succeeded in discovering in the Sherpa villages of the Solu Valley a few historical documents that appear to shed light on the circumstances surrounding the migration[2].

Shar in Tibetan means 'orient, east', and pa is the equivalent of 'man, person, people', so that one can translate shar-pa (dialectally sher-pa) as 'person from the east, people from the orient'. The name itself is a general indication that the Sherpas were originally migrants from the remote region located to the east of the Himalaya. But whence, how and when did it take place; this significant translocation of a people who would fundamentally change the population and culture of the mountain valleys of Solu and Khumbu, and other smaller valleys in the territory of present-day Nepal?

[2]Michael Oppitz, *Geschichte und Sozialordnung der Sherpa*, Khumbu Himal, vol. 8. (Innsbruck/Munich: Wagner, 1968).
Michael Oppitz, Myths and Facts: Reconsidering Some Data Concerning the Clan History of the Sherpa, in Contributions to the Anthropology of Nepal, ed. C. von Fürer-Heimendorf (University of London, Warminster: Aris and Phillips, 1974), 232-243.

The research of Michael Oppitz has proved that the migration was accomplished in two stages. The starting point was a place called Salmo Gang in Kham. From there the Sherpas moved slowly in the direction of the region in central and southern Tibet near the border with Sikkim, particularly in the areas of Tingkye and Tingri. At a later point in time there was a second, much shorter but more difficult migration, which led over the Nangpa Pass (5806 m)[3], and thence down through the Himalaya to the mountain valleys of Solu and Khumbu. It seems that the first phase of the migration was viewed by the Sherpas themselves as having taken them to their goal, and that only extremely trying conditions that arose later, and which we shall come back to below, induced their leaders to move on farther south. Why did the Sherpas leave Kham in the first place, though? And when?

As for the date, it appears that one has to go back very far, perhaps to the fourteenth century, when the pressure that the Mongols brought to bear upon the Tibetans of the north-east must have been particularly stiff and burdensome, such that it is became intolerable for some. The departure is not likely to have been a headlong flight, undertaken in a moment of hopelessness and despair. The old chronicles that Oppitz studied tell of long and well-planned preparations, of the sale of herds and houses in order to obtain gold, which was easy to transport and everywhere exchangeable. It seems, too, that the migrants (who were not all that numerous; perhaps several hundred persons) were cordially taken in by monasteries and villages along the way, since they

---

[3]Some maps give the height as 5716 m.

A Tibetan family in Kham.

conducted themselves not as vagabonds but as people who dutifully paid for goods and services. When they reached the territory between Tingkye and Tingri, their wanderings seemed to be over. Presumably the Sherpas thought that they had found a new homeland to settle, work peacefully and multiply in.

And yet something must have happenmed, for after a fair amount of time had passed, several generations later, the migration recommenced. There has been much speculation about this second move, including economic and political pressures. The Sherpas supposedly farmed land that others wanted to appropriate or had already claimed for themselves. Religious problems have also been hinted at, particularly the possibility of aggressive missionary activity on the part of the Gelug-pas (the 'virtuous ones'), members of the so-called Yellow Hat Sect (from the colour of their ritual head-covering), which was founded by the great reformer Tsong Kapa (1357-1419). We know little about the original conditions under which the Sherpas lived. It is possible that they adhered to the pre-Buddhist Bon (or Bön) religion, which was prevalent in the border regions of Tibet, and especially so in Kham and the Himalayan valleys. It is more probable, though, that they professed the older Buddhism of the Nyingma-pas, which rejected all reform and followed the teachings of the great wonder-working master Padma Sambhava (eighth century).

Now the dates become important: If the second migration occurred in the sixteenth century, as is very probable, the hypothesis of Gelug-pa pressure can only be upheld with great difficulty, since the sect was still in the process of consolidating its power at the

9

Sherpa women in Solu Khumbu.

time. It was only in the year 1578, in fact, that the senior abbot of the Gelug-pas, Sönam Gyatso ('Sea of Fame'), met with the Mongol king Atlan Khan, for what can only be called a summit (to exchange mutual assurances of deep respect and devotion [4]) at Kokonor (Chinese Chinghai, Tsinghai or Qinghai, depending on the transliteration).

The abbot was honoured with the title of Dalai ('sea', i.e. 'of wisdom'), mwhile the religious leader accorded the ruler the name King of the Faith, Exalted Purity. To be accurate, Sönam Gyatso should have been regarded as the first Dalai Lama (or Tale Lama, as the Tibetans say), but since he was the third abbot of the sect, people viewed him as the third high priest, applying the title retroactively to his predecessors. A new, powerful and sacred

dynasty of pontifical kings now arose and asserted themselves on the roof of the world.

After the early death of Sönam Gyatso in 1588, a reincarnation was discovered, with the metaphysical shrewdness of a Machiavelli, in the small great-grandson of Atlan Khan, of all people. But all things considered, the Fourth Dalai Lama, Yonten Gyatso (1589-1617) can be seen as a transitional figure, among other reasons because he died fairly young (supposedly from poison). The truly outstanding personality of the dynasty, the founder of the Tibetan theocracy familiar in the following centuries and up into recent times, was Ngawang Lobsang Gyatso ('Power of the Word, Right Inspiration, Sea [of Wisdom]'). He was born in 1617 as the reincarnation of his predecessors, and from childhood on, the great pope of the Yellow Sect, and, moreover, the earthly incarnation of the Bodhisattva Avalokiteshvara (Tibetan: Chenresig), was the personification of love and goodness. The

---

[4]D. Snellgrove and H. Richardson, A Cultural History of Tibet (London: Weidenfeld and Nicolson, 1968; Boulder: Prajna Press, 1980), 184.

Fifth Dalai Lama, the Great Fifth, as he is often called, was as important for the Tibetans as Louis XIV was for the French, Emperor Chien Lung for the Chinese, Henry VIII for the English, Philip II for the Spanish or Peter the Great for the Russians. An active man, he was clear-sighted, magnanimous when called for, but fearful and even terrifying if the occasion demanded. The country found itself being led by him towards unity, glory and true independence.

As the religious leader of the Buddhists, Ngawang Lobsang had no military force at his disposal. But he knew how to use his spiritual influence with extraordinary skill, particularly with regard to the Mongols, who were converting to Buddhism in ever-greater numbers and with ever heightened zeal.

One of their kings, Gushri Khan, worked closely with the Great Fifth and was eager to trade military protection for spiritual guidance and blessings for himself and his subjects. The territory under the rule of the Dalai Lama was now very extensive. It stretched from Kham in the east to Mount Kailasa (i.e. Mount Kailash) and even further west, almost up to the gates of Ladakh; from the mountain valleys of the Himalaya in the south up to the Kunlun Mountains in the north. It was not, to be sure, the powerful Tibetan kingdom of Tisong Detsen (755-795), but it missed being so by very little.

The Great Fifth always attached special importance to the etiquette and ceremony that glorified his position, which by now was not only that of a high priest but also of a worldly ruler. The Potala Palace in Lhasa had been the country's seat of power since the time of the old Tibetan kingdom. Many later princes of Central Tibet, both important ones and less important ones, took up residence there. Ngawang Lobsang wanted to extend and beautify

Lamas (monks) at Tengboche during the Mani Rimdu festival.

it to the utmost degree possible. Under his personal supervision, the huge complex of buildings, which contains over one thousand rooms, largely took on its present appearance. Like an enchanted Vatican-like fortress, it rises out of the rock, towering up into the sky with a richness of colour, and adorning and crowning the mountain nature gave it for a foundation.

There is a very well known portrait of Ngawang Lobsang Gyatso in the Potala Palace[5]. In general, Tibetan art is hagiographic, idealising the subjects of its portrayal in at times an exaggeratedly flattering manner. Here, however, the artist, perhaps overcome by the personality, has left us a portrait that competes in vividness and realism with the best busts of Roman emperors. The powerful jaws one can sense beneath the furrowed cheeks bespeak the energy of a man of action; the broad forehead and steady, confident look in the eyes betray unusual intelligence. The Great Fifth was, all in all, magnanimous towards the other Buddhist sects, so long as they did not oppose him too openly. And in-between one military campaign and the next, he even found time, among his various activities as religious leader, statesman, builder and charismatic ruler of his people, to author a considerable number of works, on both religious and historical topics. The extraordinary spiritual greatness of this man awoke such deep reverence among his contemporaries that his death, which occurred in 1682, was kept secret for fifteen years by his representative, Sengye Gyatso, out of fear that news of it might unleash uncontrollable unrest in the country.

---

[5][Various authors], **The Potala Palace of Tibet** (Hong Kong: Shanghai People's Art Publishing House Joint Publishing Co., 1982), 77, table 65.

12

Kapa Gyalzen mounts a prayer flag in front of his house in Khumjung.

If, therefore, the Sherpas found themselves forced to leave their home in Tibet in the sixteenth century, the reason for their emigration is not likely to be connected with religious oppression. If, on the other hand, it was the seventeenth century, most of which was dominated by the all-present, authoritarian figure of the Great Fifth, it may well have been.

Michael Oppitz ventures a theory. He recalls that Tibet was reduced to a state of terror and anxiety by the armed hordes of a fanatical Muslim king, Sultan Sa'id Khan, from 1531 to 1533. They came from Kashgar, which today lies in the territory of the Chinese province of Sinkiang (Xinjiang). The Muslims had their sights set on Lhasa, which, however, they failed to reach and destroy. But they did cause great suffering and horrific devastation in the part of Central Tibet where the Sherpas had settled. Oppitz

writes, "Assuming that this invasion by foreigners has a direct link with the flight of the Sherpas over the passes of the Himalaya into Nepal, as certain indications lead us to believe, we can date their arrival in Solu Khumbu with great exactitude. It must have been in 1533.[6]*"*

Whether this or some other later date was the fateful one, one thing is certain. The Sherpas gained a firm foothold in their new homeland, and did so in an astounding manner, by using the valleys that had previously been empty, unsettled and infertile, and turning them into a region in which people could live. They are a very small community, whose numbers are variously

[6]Oppitz, 1974, *op. cit.*, 233.

estimated by some to be 110,000, and by others 30,000, depending on the statistical criteria.

Presumably around 1600 other clans joined the original core of four exogamous clans, and still others in the hundred years between 1750 and 1850. The late arrivals, those who came between 1800 and 1850, are regarded as members of pseudo-clans. The Khampas came as the penultimate group, and at the very end were the refugees who left Tibet after 1959. Christoph von Fürer-Haimendorf counted 27 clans[7]. Living together with the genuine Sherpas, who are subdivided into many different groups, are small communities of Nepalese, particularly in the less high-lying sections of the valleys. Thus the world of the Sherpas, which may seem on the surface so simple, idyllic and rooted in bucolic traditions is, in reality, given its many layers, complex, obscure and full of pitfalls, as the first anthropologists who wished to study it in detail immediately recognised[8].

The expedition Reinhold Messner tells of in this book follows the path of the Sherpas of old in the reverse direction, leading from the south, from the valleys of Solu and Khumbu, northwards to the Nangpa La (Pass). The long ascent of the glacier makes this stretch dangerous even for well-equipped mountaineers. One is truly astounded, and reduced to admiration, to realise that a courageous group of men tackled it long ago, taking women, children, old people and domestic animals with them, and this at a time when clothing, footwear and equipment were still very simple. And in the end the Sherpas made it. They passed the test. They won the wager with destiny.

Fosco Maraini

[7]Christoph von Fürer-Haimendorf, *The Sherpas of Nepal: Buddhist Highlanders* (London: Murray, 1964; reprint 1972), 19.

[8]See particularly S. B. Ortner, *Sherpas through Their Rituals* (Cambridge: Cambridge University Press, 1978).

The Way to Cho Oyu

Thame (the monastery is rust-red) with the surrounding villages in Solu Khumbu. In the upper right: the all-over-towering Cho Oyu. A yak caravan is descending from the Nangpa La. Sherpas are seen below Tashi Laptsa.

Cho Oyu is the name of one of the mountains on the border between Tibet and Nepal. The Tibetan name has been translated as 'Goddess of Turquoise'. [1] Page 4

The Sherpas, 'the People from the East', inhabit the sparsely covered mountain pastures to the south of this eight-thousand-metre peak; to the north live Tibetans. Directly to the west of Cho Oyu, the sturdiest men of the Himalaya have been plying back and forth since earliest memory across the Nangpa La, a pass nearly six thousand metres high, in order to carry on trade. The Sherpas obtain salt and wool in Tibet, and the Tibetans exchange yaks for cloth or barley in Solu Khumbu.

When the Chinese central government proclaimed its sovereignty over the Tibetan plateau, and the Dalai Lama, in 1959, left Lhasa, this crossing was closed. The Himalaya became an impassable frontier barrier between two related peoples.

------

[1] As G. O. Dyhrenfurth (To the Third Pole [London: 1955], 120) noted, the meaning of the name Cho Oyu is far from clear. It may correspond in written Tibetan to the term jomo-yu, but the grammatical form is ambiguous. Judging by the form that has come down to us, the name is more likely to mean 'Turquoise of the Goddess' or 'Divine Turquoise'.

Cho Oyu from the south, with the base camp of the winter expedition. The South Tyrolean expedition of 1982 failed in an ascent of the south-east slope (to the right of the fall line from the summit).

Over a period of ten years I had often been to Solu Khumbu, having lived for weeks with the Sherpas in Khumjung and having listened for hours to the singsong of the lamas in Tengboche.[2] I had been to Ama Dablam and on top of Mount Everest. Twice I had been in close proximity to Cho Oyu from the Tibetan side; once having come from Rongbuk, and once from Tingri. It had never been possible for me to make it all the way to the Nangpa La, not even in December 1982, when I attempted a winter ascent of this sacred mountain of Nepal with a South Tyrolean expedition. It would be another half year before I would be standing on this history-filled site for the first time. The government of Nepal had again offered me permission to climb Cho Oyu, this time from the Nangpa La.

When we set off in April 1983 for the attempted ascent, Cho Oyu had the distinction of being the least climbed of the eight-thousand-metre peaks. There were three of us; Hans Kammerlander, who, in a winter attempt, had made it to within one day from the top; Michl Dacher, who wanted an eight-thousand-metre peak for his fiftieth birthday; and me. Plus we had five Sherpas, one to cook, one to fetch the mail from the valley each week, and three to re-supply the base camp.

----

[2]This is the correct name of the monastery, a transcription of sTeng-bo-che, 'High, Broad Place'. The spelling Tyangboche or Thyangboche is wrong according to Snellgrove, even though it appears on the maps of the Ordinance Survey of India. See D. Snellgrove, *Buddhist Himalaya* (Oxford: Bruno Cassirer, 1957), 317.

Trekkers in Solu-Khumbu. To the right: Cho Oyu in the background,
its south-east slope to the right and its mysterious south-west
slope to the left, under the clouds.

We selected a new approach from the southwest. I didn't want to climb this peak just to chalk up another mountaineering success. I was in search of a mystery; the mythic power that pervades the highest regularly crossed pass in the world, and the meaning of the mountain that transfigures and overshadows this crossing. Whence came the faith of the people who lived on the hither and further sides of the great snow-covered chain, and who felt protected by the mountains?

It was the middle of April. The trekkers who came back from the mountains to the capital Kathmandu were radiant. Some told of how they had been held back by impassable drifts of snow; others described the cold nights up in the mountains. All complained of the winter weather. Nevertheless, their faces were tanned, their looks full of rapture over the Himalaya.

On the street a hundred metres away I could tell apart a trekker and one of those who had come to Nepal for some warm days a few weeks before the monsoon. Another sort still were the many tourists there to try something different for a change, who never ceased proclaiming what they had seen and heard; purveyors of religion pure and simple. They accosted you at every street crossing, in every restaurant, just when you wanted some peace.

I had a real urge now to head out into the stormy afternoon sky. Distant clouds towered up to the west of the city. The dark forested hills beneath them were almost black. Lightning flashed intermittently. Hardly any thunder. Showers flitted across the land in waves.

I was happy to have everything under control, to be on the road. I went back to Cho Oyu, even though I had failed to reach the top a few months earlier. I went where the water sources were still sacred, the forests still mysterious, and the mountains so tall that people were afraid of them.

Pictures were, when all was said and done, pictures. Reality might look entirely different. Not following others' advice (that you must see, there is where you should go) but going where no one had yet gone was the attraction of this trip. Delving into the unknown was the goal. Thus I feverishly yearned to be on the flight from Kathmandu into the mountains.

The real Himalayas began an hour from the capital. Far below, in a gorge wedged between black mountains and the Dudh Kosi River, lay the Sherpa village of Lukla. Emil Wick circled around twice with his Pilatus Porter. There was the landing field; stony, encased within two fences and a cluster of people at the upper edge of it. Nearby stood wooden huts misshapen by the wind (most of them with corrugated iron roofing); in them tea and rice beer were served.

Each time it was a stunt just to land the plane safely on this steep strip. Taking off was even more difficult. There was no better pilot than Emil Wick in Nepal. I could feel completely at ease.

In Lukla I searched out two-dozen porters, and two hours later we headed off. In spite of the drizzle.

Further up the valley I saw remains of a recent snowfall in the cloud-enshrouded clumps of trees. It had snowed down to below the three-thousand-metre level. The people who hurried in groups to the Saturday market in Namche Bazaar were drenched to the bone. Many of these porters had surely been on their feet since before dawn. A piece of bamboo plaiting the size of a tablecloth was just enough to cover their baskets, which were filled with vegetables, meat, fruit or eggs, and which they carried with the help of a tumpline.

A winter scene in Solu Khumbu.
The expedition caravan is at the same height as Namche Bazaar. The view is towards Mount Everest (to the left, with clouds) and Ama Dablam (middle).

A bit below Namche Bazaar it began to snow. Heavy, thick flakes blew in front of my opened umbrella. None the less, a hundred or more Sherpa women crowded into the Saturday market. Some had come from afar to buy supplies; rice, vegetables, meat. I closed the umbrella and wedged my way through the people. Sitting under sheets of plastic, the traders from Solu Valley offered their wares. Their jackets dripped, and the children, who stood between them with crossed arms, shivered throughout their whole bodies. The ground was so muddy that every step produced a splash.

I went the few steps necessary into the first Sherpa hotel. Namche Bazaar was a nexus of tourist activity. Everyone and everything was geared to trekkers and mountain climbers. We were the ones responsible for everything under the sun here: corrugated iron roofs, shops with 'guaranteed genuine' Tibetan kitsch from Hong Kong, beer; a discotheque had even recently opened up.

Ravens were perched between the prayer flags on the gables of houses, sated by the garbage they retrieved on the path behind both natives and foreigners.

I sat down next to a fire in a wooden hut furnished with a few stairs and tables and ordered a chai. This milk tea tasted sweet, but otherwise like dishwater. At least it was hot. The shopkeeper said offhandedly that she was from Tibet.

Outside it was still snowing. I loathed the thought of sticking even a toe out.

This hamlet, consisting of thirty stone houses and an equal number of potato fields, was made out to be the capital of Sherpaland. The way from it led on to the right to Tengboche monastery and thence to Mount Everest; to the left, it went to Thame monastery and on to the Nangpa La. It was windy here; uncomfortable day in and day out. Namche Bazaar offered no special view and lacked the flair of other Sherpa villages such as Khumjung, Kunde or even Pangboche.

Tingri and (in the background to the right) Cho Oyu.
Sherpas with yak caravans are ascending in the direction of the Nangpa La.
Some typically dark yak-hair tents are seen between the Tibetans' houses.

Later Hans and Michl showed up, and we warmed ourselves at a fire in the kitchen.

All Sherpa families originally come from Tibet the old woman went on to say. On the eastern border of the Tibetan plateau, where the mountains form a natural barrier to Chinese Szechwan, is the province of Kham, where the Sherpas lived over five hundred years ago. We owned a lot of land in an area called Salmo Gang between the rivers feeding into the Yangtse and the Huangho.[3] Then the Sherpa clans came here.

253I had read that at the beginning of the sixteenth century they sold all their immovable property in Kham and left their homeland together with their yaks, kit and caboodle. Loaded down with household utensils, fire-gilt bronzes, silver and valuable items of clothing, they moved towards the southwest over a period of months.

Their flight took them to Lhasa, where the hierarchy of the Dalai Lamas had since been established, and then, by way of Gyangtse and Shegar Dzong, to Tingri, a large plain to the north of the sacred mountain Tseringma[4] and the all-over-towering Cho Oyu. There they long remained, in black tents, together with their herds of yaks. They visited the shrines of Rongshar at the foot of the Divine Mother, Tseringma, the daughter of the mountain god Himachal,[5] and the famous lama monastery of Rongbuk[6] on the

---

[3] A problem involving modern Chinese toponomy arises in the case of these names. The region, which was once called Szechwan or Szu-ch'uan ('The Four Rivers'), is in today's official transliteration (pinyin) written Sichuan. The two other names, those of the large rivers, are Yangzi jiang (Yangtse) and Huang (Huangho).

[4] The name Tseringma appears to mean literally 'Mother of Long Life'.

[5] Himachal, formed from hima (snow) and achal (mountain), is a synonym for the Himalaya. The term is found, among other places, in Himachal Pradesh (Himalayan State), the name of one of the most important regions in North India.

[6] According to Snellgrove, one of the most important Tibetologists of our day, the name Rongbuk, which has by now been accepted as traditional, goes back to an error in transliteration that found its way onto the maps of the Survey of India. The correct name of this monastery is rDza-rong-phu ('Clayey valley-head'). It is thus named in the official history and is so called locally. (D. Snellgrove, op. cit., 213). The abbreviated form Rong-phu would thus be more correct than Rong-buk.

An (idealised) stupa in the centre of Namche Bazaar. Satellite peaks of Mount Everest and Cho Oyu tower up in the background. At the foot of the stupa can be seen a row of prayer wheels.

river running north of Chomolungma, the 'Divine Wind Mother',[7] as they call the mountain we have dubbed Mount Everest.

After several years in the plain of Tingri, the leaders of the Sherpa clans decided to move on. There were not enough fields and pastureland for the inhabitants of Tingri, the yak-herding nomads who always spent the winter there, and the newcomers from Kham. There was strife, among other reasons because the divine kings in Lhasa were bent upon extending their religious and political power over all Tibet. The freedom-loving clans from Kham were attached to their old Bon religion and wanted nothing to do with the central government in Lhasa. The story was like a fairytale. The Sherpas crossed the Nangpa La between Tseringma and Cho Oyu, and descended by way of Lunak and Thame to Namche Bazaar. That's how they became settled here and further south in the valleys of Solu.

Namche Bazaar was filthy in the way no other village in Solu Khumbu was, particularly now in April, when the mixture of wet snow and yak dung and urine covered the dirt paths. Nonetheless, the place had for a week been an assembly point for all the trekkers whom the late snowfall had driven from the villages higher up. The hotels, the name the creakiest hut with corrugated iron roofing calls itself, were overflowing.

This caused a serious problem for us, since our liaison officer required quartering. He either couldn't or wouldn't go on, and promised to remain in Namche Bazaar for the duration of the expedition. Once it stopped snowing, the four of us went in search of a room.

All sorts of things were being sold along the way; tea, souvenirs, fruit, meat and porter services. Sherpa women were nursing their children; porters were sleeping on the ground in front of the huts. A group of young Sherpas already drunk in the morning were blocking our way. Did they know a place for us to room? One of them extended his tongue towards a medium-to-large house along the way.

There was room for all of us. We decided to stay, for a few rupees a night.

---

[7] Chomolungma (or Chomolangma or Jomolangma and other forms) means 'Divine Mother of the Village / Country / Region'. Chomo (or Jomo) means 'goddess, deity' but may be taken as the equivalent of 'mother'. The syllable lung means 'wind' in its written form rlung, but 'village, region, country etc.', and sometimes even 'world', in the form lung. The name thus conveys the meaning 'Divine Mother of the Village / World'. The name must be a fairly old one; it appears on a map of the Jesuit d'Anville from the year 1733, drawn on the basis of information supplied by Italian missionaries who lived in Lhasa from 1707 to 1733. It is easily recognisable on it, in the form Tschoumou Lancma.

Khumjung and (upper left) Thame with its Hillary Hospital (pale roof).
To the right: Mount Everest and Ama Dablam in the background. In the middle:
the rugged cliffs of Khumbila. Gyalzen's house is in the top row,
to the right of the main monastery.

For several hours now the Sherpa family above us had been stirring around, and outside I heard the whistling of the yak herders. It was not only the wretched weather; a kind of inertia and the clammy thin air kept us in our sleeping bags longer than usual. I lay there for an hour, during which, in my dream world, I was unable, though aware of them, to register the strange sounds as such. I enjoyed the delightful warmth of the sleeping bag and looked from time to time, without properly opening my eyes, towards the sky, which raced by in stormily sombre billows. We had slept deeply, even though unaccustomed to the hard floor and cramped sleeping bags.

The sky still loured grey above me, but it seemed less threatening than the day before. At least it wasn't snowing. Lying in my sleeping bag and looking through the window past the eaves, I was able to follow the path the clouds were taking. The wind was coming from the northwest. The winter, therefore, was still with us. We wanted to slip in a day of rest and use it to visit Kapa Gyalzen[8]

in Khumjung. This Sherpa naïve painter, who had accompanied me to Mount Everest to record the expedition as he saw it, and with the means he had at hand, was to come along this time too. I slowly tramped up the steep path above Namche Bazaar. The snowed-in village lay in a semicircle below us, like a deformed chessboard. When the sun came out for a moment, everything shone so brightly that my eyes hurt. Children ran back and forth between the one-storey stone houses.

Gyalzen, a thickset, deeply religious man, lived with his family in one of the narrow whitewashed houses at the upper eastern end of the neatly laid-out village. A sturdy twenty-foot-tall prayer flag fluttered in front of the main door. Gyalzen's two small daughters, who recognised me from afar, announced my arrival with shrills.

---

[8] The name means 'Victory Banner' and recalls one of the eight auspicious signs. See P. Lindegger, Onomasticon Tibetanum (Rikon: Tibet-Institut, 1976), 44.

In Gyalzen's pictures, the mountains appear to be personified. For him, even the avalanche slope, which looks like a monster and is larger than the eight-thousand-metre peak, has a soul.

Yangle, Gyalzen's lovely wife, had hot tea ready for me when I entered. I sat on the terrace between the storeroom and kitchen cum living room. In his demure manner, Gyalzen tried to explain to me that these mountains were special places, that they harboured a great deal of energy. Storms formed in them with thunder and lightning; storms came from them; avalanches buried everything that got in their way. Not a man alive was a match for these mountains. I looked into the thin mist that was now creeping up the gorge of the Dudh Kosi and settling down in every depression, until only the peaks of Thamserku, Kwangde and Khumbila were left. Their filigreed ridges stood out against the clear evening sky. The milk-blue of the firmament heightened the snow-blue of the mountain peaks into inscrutability.

These mountains, visible from far and wide, were the true deities of the Sherpas. They were orientation points in these unspeakably grand surroundings, a measure of the infinite and incomprehensible.

Gyalzen sat in the window frame and painted. Years ago he had set up a studio of sorts in his tiny room in back of the living room, with a cupboard for the finished pictures, a house altar and a bench on which carpets from Tibet lay.

Gyalzen was obviously less impressed by this spectacle of nature than I was. For him not only these peaks were divine; everything around him was holy; the earth, the forest, the water.

The Khumbu region with the Himalayan chain in the background. To the left of centre, Cho Oyu; to the right, Mount Everest, standing high above everything else. The monastery town in the foreground is Tengboche, now one of the Sherpas' religious centres.

Protected by the natural walls of the Himalayan Mountains, a way of life and a religion were being kept alive that were older than those of reformed Lamaist Tibet. Older perhaps than the Sherpa people, as old as the people in the land of snows; the Bon religion with its good and evil spirits, nature deities, sorcerers and miracle-working healers. Similarities with the intuitive knowledge of the Indians impressed themselves upon me.

Gyalzen lived wholly in the tradition of the Sherpas. He was able to tell me much of their customs. In the northeast of Nepal there were eighteen different Sherpa clans. Sherpas lived not only to the southwest of Mount Everest but also in the Kulung region at the foot of Makalu and in the Langtang-Helambu region to the north of Kathmandu. Each group spoke a Tibetan dialect all its own. They also used the Tibetan script, so that there were scarcely any problems for the Sherpas and Tibetans to understand one another.

In the language of the Sherpas, shar means 'east', and pa denotes 'people'. The Sherpas were thus the 'People from the East', coming as they did from the province of Kham, from the eastern part of Tibet.

No one, not even Gyalzen, knew precisely whether they had followed the command of a leader in trekking from Kham to the Solu Khumbu region, or were driven off by the Mongol hordes. Someone trusting to visions and oracles had shown them the way south-west. Perhaps they had left because of religious differences.

The knowledge of this long period of wandering had remained alive in the consciousness of many families. These Sherpas had moved about within Tibet for two generations before finding a new homeland to the south of the Himalaya. The fathers had set off in Salmo in Kham; it was only the grandsons who would arrive in Solu Khumbu in Nepal.

Why was it here of all places that the Sherpa clans came? How could they know in Kham of these valleys, of these mountains? Since time untold this region had been of mystical significance for the Sherpas, and perhaps for all Tibetans. The Buddhist mystics Milarepa and Padmasambhava had meditated here; from here magic powers emanated.

There was no doubting that Solu Khumbu was set among one of the most beautiful landscapes on earth. For as long as no roads had been built here, for as long as there were neither mines nor dammed lakes, nature had remained in equilibrium. This intuitive striving for harmony in everything suffused the life of these people. This came out in their work, and expressed itself in their prayers and in all of their customs.

Gyalzen's house was already bustling early in the morning. The prayer flags in front of the house had to be replaced; a ceremony lasting several hours. An impression was first set on an approximately six-metre-long and forty-centimetre-wide flag made from a kind of coarse muslin. The necessary print blocks, with alphabetic characters and figures, came from Tengboche monastery, the holy place from which Mount Everest, Lhotse and Ama Dablam are visible.

While Gyalzen went about nailing the new prayer flags to the eight-metre-tall mast in front of the house, Yangle lit a sacrificial fire on the terrace abutting on the eastern side of the house.

I helped Gyalzen to raise the pole. We wedged it in place with stones. Then we left the house, having first emptied a glass of chang, and went to Täsho, whence the expedition was scheduled to continue the next day.

We carefully kept our balance along the narrow path through Khumjung. Melting water trickled everywhere. Children stood in the low house entrances. At least one woman from each house was looking out of the window.

The sun shone brightly; Everest and Lhotse stood darkly, forming a background to the valley. The winter storm had swept clear the southern slopes down to the rock.

Not only the mountains but also the forests are full of mystery for the Sherpas. There the gods reside. In the picture; yaks and dogs (Tibetan mastiffs) around two nomad tents.

Just beyond Syangboche we plunged into thick forest. The Sherpas were afraid of this mountain jungle. Gyalzen passed through it, a kingdom of spirits and demons, in religious awe.

The Sherpas had not known such humid mountain forests in their former homeland of Kham. But just as the sweep of the Tibetan high plateau with its snow and sandstorms harboured uncanny power, so too these murky tropical forests were now for them full of natural forces whose names could not be uttered.

We strove on at a fast pace towards Täsho, a small hamlet halfway between Namche Bazaar and Thame. Rhododendron bushes were blooming here and there. The large-leafed trees towered up to twenty metres into the blue-grey of the morning fog. We needed less than an hour on the wide footpath with aromatic pines right and left to reach the house of Ang Dorje,[9] who was to accompany us as our Sherpa guide.

It was here somewhere, years ago, that Ang Dorje had seen a yeti, one of the Abominable Snowmen. Fear flickers over his face even today when he tells of it. The wild man had come from out of the cliffs and had jumped on to the path in front of him. It was about one and a half metres tall, and blacker than night. On all fours it had crossed the torrent, a stream, at a spot where no Sherpa would have dared to do so.

Our sirdar was waiting for us at the house entrance. A loud welcoming. We didn't see any yeti, I said to Ang Dorje.

'The yeti lives', he answered, 'but you'll never see him. You'll only see traces of him.'

Ang Dorje had ordered yaks, but it was only the next day that the trek proceeded up to Marulung, where Dorje owned a mountain pasture that he wished to put at our disposal for a few nights.

---

[9] Dorje (Dorjee) is one of the commonest names for men, both in Tibet and among the Sherpas. Dorje means 'lightning' and 'diamond'; further, it signifies a well-known liturgical device used by the lamas of all sects during their rites.

PASANG NURBU KHUM JUNG

Täsho, the site of Ang Dorje's house. To the right there is a large boulder. Prayer flags can be seen on all houses. The mountains in the background block the view of Cho Oyu.

Dorje's premises, a small piece of property between boulders the size of a house, looked like land that had been wrested from the primeval forest a matter of years earlier; the potato fields full of stones, everywhere tree trunks, the nearby stream unharnessed. When I asked Ang Dorje why he didn't cultivate his land, he only shook his head. That's the way things were, and were meant to be. The gods wanted it so. A balance of natural forces had to be maintained. Any interference with this ordered state would have endangered life-giving forces. Sources of water remained untouched, rubbish was not thrown into the fire, stones were not blown apart.

In the morning the world was aglow; snow as far as we could see. Water and snow had frozen together into a hard crust in front of the house and along paths. The yaks stepped more carefully than they usually did. They came from every direction, perhaps twelve in number, and the Sherpas whistled them on from behind. Joining in with these porters, we set the loads on the animals. Then we set off. From the broadly splayed toes on their feet I could see that the porters had not been wearing shoes for years.

Such days have nothing of the drudgery, nothing of the danger, of mountain climbing. I sensed the earnestness of our undertaking only from a yearning for a greater sense of familiarity.

Thame under snow. To the upper right: the monastery. The yak, an extremely versatile animal that provides wool and fuel (dung) along with meat and milk, has to be fed only after large snowfalls.

In Thame, Hans and I used our lead to visit the monastery. This monastery of lamas, even though founded little more than sixty years ago, is one of the Sherpas' religious centres.

The Sherpas are Buddhists; they belong to the Kagyu-pa school. That is the oldest sect of Lamaism. For them, the practice of religion is as much a matter of course as harvesting potatoes and drinking tea. Even as Nature and God are one, so too are work and prayer, while cult offerings are for farmer and lama alike an element of their religious ritual. But the rhythm of Sherpa life also has its roots in the Bon religion and in local animism. Gods and demons live in caves, forests and streams, and on the highest mountain peaks.[10]

In Thame, the highest permanent settlement below the Nangpa La, there were cultivated fields of barley and potatoes.

In the middle of the village a young Sherpa woman was cutting an old man's hair with sheep shears.

Ang Dorje had in the meantime put himself up with relatives. The latter invited us, too, to have some potatoes and chang. There was nothing else here to eat. Along with barley and vegetables, they formed the staple diet of the Sherpa families in remote villages.

Two hours later we pulled ourselves away. We headed uphill between breast-high stone walls that enclosed fields the size of a room.

The caravan of porters and yaks was ahead of us. Three Tibetans who came toward us, their backs bent from the years of supporting loads, looked at us in disbelief. Nangpa La? My inquisitiveness elicited no response, only an uncomprehending shake of the head. From their mud-stained shoes, however, I realised that they had come from far away.

---

[10] The temple and monastery of Rongphu at the foot of Mount Everest on the Tibetan side of the border may be regarded as the cradle of all important religious institutions among the Sherpas: the monasteries of Tengboche and Thame in Khumbu, and those of Chiwong, Takshindo and Tsodukpa in Solu. The abbots of Rongphu monastery are looked upon as reincarnations of the Bodhisattva Vajrapani (Tib. Chanadorje). The sixth of these reincarnated abbots, a half-legendary figure from the distant past, the lama Sanga Dorje, is viewed by the Sherpas as the missionary who propagated Buddhism among them.
See C. von Fürer-Haimendorf, The Sherpas of Nepal: Buddhist Highlanders (London: John Murray, 1964; reprint: 1972), 127; and S. B. Ortner, Sherpas through Their Rituals. (Cambridge: Cambridge University Press, 1978), 30.

The highland pasture of Maruhung with the expedition tents. The individual fields, pastures and potato plots are separated from one another by stone walls.

We had set up two tents in Marulung and now watched the snow dissipate. On the second day of rest we were witness to a religious ceremony that Ang Dorje wished to have performed without fail before our further ascent.

Three times a year, Ang Dorje said, he dedicated his house, his goods and his family to the gods. Today was a good day for him. We couldn't go forward without conducting this sacrifice. Already in the early hours of the morning we could hear the singsong of our Sherpas. Together with the blue smoke, it forced its way out of every crevice of the hut. Later a magician arrived, a lama from Thame. Schooled by the nature gods, he was the only person who could instruct men in their dealings with the spirits.

An altar had been erected in the hut, with small butter lamps, a thangka and various offerings: rice, a wooden flask of chang, brushwood. Hour after hour the lama sat with Ang Dorje in front of the altar. They recited prayers. We drank chang. Eye-stinging smoke billowed. Ang Dorje threw aromatic herbs into the fire.

The Sherpas of Khumjung and Thame changed their prayer flags three times a year. While doing so, they prayed to various gods.

In Khumjung they worshipped Khumbila. This was the same name as the steep, dark mountain that rose up above the village. Here they turned to Cho Oyu, meaning by this name not the mountain; gods and mountains were one.

There were three words that recurred over and over during the endless litany; Khumbila, Cho Oyu, Nangbigobataia.[11] When I asked Ang Dorje whether these deities were identical with the mounta3ins, he slapped his hand against his forehead, laughing and shaking his head. Such a grand allegory could have passed muster only in the solitude of the Himalaya. The Goddess of Turquoise really did exist.

---

[11] This name may refer to the god Khumbu-yülka, which is mentioned by Fürer-Haimendorf, op. cit., 127 and passim. It may also derive from Nangpai (genitive of Nangpa, Nangpa Pass) or from jo-va-ta-ya, an exclamation of joy: reaching the pass, people let out cries of joy, often with no fixed meaning.
In any case, it is certain that the mountains are in most cases holy in the eyes of Sherpas and Tibetans alike, being either the homes of gods or even the gods themselves.
On the holy mountains in Tibet, see D. Snellgrove & H. Richardson, A Cultural History of Tibet (London: Weidenfeld & Nicolson, 1968; Boulder [Colorado]: Prajna Press, 1980) as well as R. A. Stein: La Civilisation tibétaine (Paris: Dunod, 1962).

Ang Dorje in the process of changing prayer flags on the roof of his pasture hut in Maruhung. In the foreground: his wife and his twenty-year-old-plus lead yak.

Fog was clearing from the valley as Ang Dorje changed the prayer flags on his house roof. He tied one blue, one white, one red, one green and one yellow pennon each on the bamboo poles. The blue at the very top symbolised heaven, the firmament; the white, the clouds; the red, fire; the green, water and life; the yellow earth. I asked no questions, only observed; how he pierced tiny holes in the ears of a goat, how he attached prayer flags to them, how he rubbed fat over its horns.

This goat was also a god, ever since the world had existed. Through many reincarnations it had come from Tibet to Sherpa land. When it died, Ang Dorje looked for its reincarnation; the same way the Dalai Lama was found. He would buy the goat and keep it as something sacred. Ang Dorje pronounced 'goat' and 'god' exactly the same. They were the same thing for him too.

The mixture of mumbling and talk between drunken men died out in the evening. For Ang Dorje a tiring day had come to an end; he was supremely happy. Now he was armed against any buffets fate might hold in store.

As we walked in the moonlight from the pasture hut to our tents, the valley seemed to be further off. As if the mountains had retreated. Beneath us stood a dozen or so stone huts, small and large, and between them a low wall and the remains of snow; every-thing icily cold in the moon's night light. Now we would be heading into completely isolated areas, along the route that was for the Sherpas the door to their new homeland five hundred years ago.

Yak caravans on the way to Cho Oyu. Each animal carries two containers weighing 25 kilos apiece. The Sherpas are whistling them on.

We wanted to set off at eight o'clock. It was already ten by the time the yaks were loaded. We were bid farewell with a cup of chang. Slowly we ascended behind the pack animals, along a stretch of land chequered white and brown. We remained throughout on the orographically left side of the valley, passing the last summer settlements of Lungare and Arye.

Thick clouds thrust their way out of the valley earlier than on the previous days. Anxious that snow might fall (it was only early afternoon), the yak drivers pressed us to call a halt. We set up camp on a broad field of snow, probably an abandoned pasture at the edge of the Nangpa Glacier. The melancholy that is unique to such places overcame even me. A stone hut stood uninhabited; behind it, a stone's throw away, began the rugged glacier. Once the tents were up, all the porters had a place to stay, and the yaks had been given their hay, the three of us lay down in out tents.

I fantasised to myself how the route ahead would be; Cho Oyu rose up before me like a vision. No one in the world knew whether the peak could be climbed from here or not.

When I looked out of the tent to see how the weather was, thick fog was rolling over us. The view was miserable. Far off, in the background, white pieces of mountain projected up out of the cloud-enclosed valley. Ridges and fog towered up like a foretaste of Cho Oyu.

Cho Oyu from the south. Rocks, rises and, above all, the summit serve as orientation points not only for the Sherpas but also for mountain climbers.

With such visibility we would have found neither Cho Oyu nor the Nangpa La. We had no choice but to wait; wait until the weather was better. These hours of uncertainty were a kind of religious training.

The fog thinned in the evening, but the valley was still full of clouds. The only place where the sky was clear and open was where we wanted to go. For a while the flare of dusk turned the harsh mountain world into the kitsch of a theatre backdrop.

What a morning that was! Even before the sky turned grey, I heard the regular thud of snow on the tent canvas. I knew everything there was to know when Joganath brought the tea at seven o'clock. We couldn't go on. The yak drivers tramped the way out the valley to fetch hay. There was no pasture owing to the heavy winter snowfall, and the animals had to feed.

We stared into the grey fog. It was only as we were writing a few letters, crouched in our tents, that we each managed to forget the others. For a few hours we traded the world around us for thoughts of home.

Following another cold night, Joganath brought the morning tea with the news, 'Good weather, Sahib.' Indeed, the sky was blue; we could head on.

The way to Lunak was long. The yak caravan took so long to get under way that I was driven to desperation. In places the snow lay a metre deep; snowdrifts from the winter months.

The three of us now went first, beating out a path in the snow. The yaks followed.

Walking the whole day in the sun, with the wind in my face, had a calming effect. Even though we had not come all that far, things were moving.

The sun was sinking as we came to a halt in Lunak at the site of a half dozen stone shelters. Evening shadows flooded the valleys. Bizarre mountain shapes formed the backdrop to the valleys. A sudden burst of wind ripped away the sleeping bags we had hung on the tent tops to dry. The Sherpas yelled and dove after them. None of us thought the next day that we would ever reach Kanchung with the yaks. The snow was several metres deep in the depressions, and the animals wouldn't budge. Often we needed more than an hour to go one hundred metres. During the afternoon we remained with the drivers when heavy snowfall again set in. In this way we kept the yaks from fleeing.

In the grey between snowdrifts and night we entered Kanchung. It was not the base camp we had planned, being too low and far too distant from the Nangpa La, but failure was for the time being postponed.

The base camp in Kanchung. Above, signalled by its prayer flags, is the Nangpa La. To the right is Nangpa Gotai, the horse-head mountain.

Three days were spent setting up camp. Ang Dorje took meticulous care that no garbage was burned in it and that no one spat in the fire. We camped directly under Nangpa Gotai, the sacred mountain Hayagriva, whose peak had the shape of a horse's head. This inconspicuous mass of rock did not surpass six thousand metres, but still it was among the holiest of mountains for the Sherpas. Nangpa Gotai always cropped up with Khumbila and Cho Oyu in the conversations of our escorts. A cult to a nature god was being practised here that we could make only faint sense of.[12]

From Kanchung onwards only humans and yaks could continue the climb; every horse that had tried to cross the Nangpa La had died in Kanchung, our camping site. This is what Ang Dorje told us. The yak is the most intelligent of animals; it could go higher. We remained one week at the base camp, at the foot of the mountain with the head of a horse. From all the gestures the Sherpas made I realised that Nangpa Gotai was God in this region. All gods were confined to a geographically fixed territory; they were by nature local. It would have been wrong to see them in universal terms.

The downpour of hail ended abruptly. A jagged bank of clouds moved off to the east. The sun broke through and brought back a festive mood to our colourful assemblage.

'And even if we need a whole month, and it's all no use, we'll give it a go.' The expedition went on. Just for the sake of it.

---

[12] Tamdrin (Sanskrit: Hayagriva) is a very old deity that Buddhism adopted from Hinduism. The name means 'Horse-headed'. Indeed, the god is easily recognisable from the small horse's head he wears in his hair. Tamdrin/Hayagriva is first and foremost a tutelary deity.

He appears in many forms. Generally he is wild and excitable, or else he assumes a terrifying appearance. He may be seen alone or in mystical coitus with his female energy (shakti). His preferred colour is red.

See A. Getty: The Gods of Northern Buddhism (Oxford: Clarendon Press, 1928; Tokyo: Tuttle, 1963), 162.

The next morning the three Sherpas were supposed to climb to the Nangpa La in order to set up a depot there.

Hans and I were convinced that we would make it up the mountain in alpine fashion by having a forward base camp. Only Michl was in a state of despair. He rushed from tent to tent, from the kitchen to me, from me to Hans, as if he alone were capable of forestalling the collapse of the expedition. What caused him to doubt success was perhaps the fact that he was alone in his tent, on the evening that seemed to plunge everything into gloom.

I was still half asleep when Joganath began rummaging around in the kitchen. It may have been around five o'clock. The familiar sound of tins and his dry cough penetrated my ears, in between steps over hard-frozen snow.

Simultaneously murmurings arose in the Sherpa tent and, after frequent clearings of throats, crescendoed to a singsong. Ang Dorje launched into prayer; Phurba and Ang Khami repeated his words. At the time the sky was still covered with veils of cloud. In the half-light of dawn, the moon had set, the sun lit only the silhouettes in the east; the breaking day had a macabre effect on me.

Two hours later we were breakfasting in the sun. The last wisp of white cloud had disappeared. Joganath served tea, chapatis and fried eggs.

Far above, where the icefall began, pushing its way through the rubble like the scaly armour of a huge dinosaur, three tiny points could be seen: the Sherpas who had climbed to set up our depot close to the Nangpa La.

Ang Dorje, Phurba and Ang Khami returned around noon, tired but content. They had seen tracks at the pass, but not a single person far and wide.

A yak caravan descending from the Nangpa La. Cho Oyu towers up to the right. This Himalayan pass is still used to transport trade goods from Tibet to Nepal and vice-versa.

The morning of April 28 was again cloudless. Hour after hour the wild north-west wind out of Tibet cleared the sky clean. Everything seemed nearer than in the days before. The sky had something corporeal about it; a bad sign weatherwise.

The wind changed course while it was still morning. It came from the valley, thrusting the fog out in front of it. Soon every nook and cranny in the mountains was full.

Around noontime two figures came into view beneath the Nangpa Glacier. They were coming downhill. With a pair of binoculars we could see that they were carrying large backpacks. Their clothing was dark, their gait slow. They took far more breaks that would have been customary for Sherpas or Tibetans.

Who were these men? What were they up to? Was it possible that they had plundered our depot at the Nangpa La?

During our ascent from Marulung to our present position we had noticed here and there footprints covered with snow, and the next day four men had crossed the Nangpa La from Nepal to Tibet.

I waited in front of the tent for the mysterious figures. When they showed up I did not succeed in getting them to halt. I offered them tea; invited them in. The two fellows slinked on past the camp as if they had a hoard of stolen goods on their backs. They didn't stop. Obviously they were smugglers. When one of them did stop for a few breaths, Ang Dorje recognised him. He was a Sherpa from Thame. Perhaps they had accompanied two Tibetans to the other side of the Nangpa La.

58

We gave ourselves time. Nothing is more dangerous and stupid at high altitudes than spending yourself. We went over the rutted Nangpa Glacier up to beneath the icefall and then to the right over some steps to the smooth glacial stream, which stretched out in a broad S up to the watershed.

The carcasses of yaks lay in narrow crevasses. Avalanches threatened from the right. One dead yak hung spectrally from an ice tower. It had plunged down years earlier, and the ice around the desiccated body had evaporated.

When the Sherpas had first come south, they had come over this pass between Cho Oyu and Tseringma. Here was the exact place they had crossed the Himalaya. It was unbelievable; five hundred years ago entire Sherpa clans had supposedly walked over this pass with children and yak caravans! The wind, the crevasses, the thin air! The gods must have been with them. It must be that Nature adapts to the needs of the weakest; she offers protection to those who trust themselves to her.

It took some four hours to climb from the base camp up to the forward camp. We had sunk the tents approximately fifty centimetres into the snow, so that the feared northwest wind could not simply topple them. Such a camp just below the Nangpa La was to my liking. There, one yellow and one blue tent stood in an expansive field of snow, slightly inclined towards Nepal. The clouds passed across the deep-blue sky like small ships. Northwards, in the direction of Tibet, it seemed as if the world would further open up.

60

The towering Cho Oyu from the north. China, which occupies Tibet, now also grants permits to climb the mountain from the other side.

We still did not know how we would be able to climb Cho Oyu. The crossing by way of the Nangpa La was off limits to us. The Chinese, who controlled Tibet, kept a close watch on the border. The time to decide was approaching quickly. We had to climb a narrow notch on Nangpai Gosum that, like a window, provided an unobstructed view onto the untrodden southwest slope of Cho Oyu. We had but little acclimatised ourselves, and time was also pressing.

The notch up to Nangpai Gosum posed no problem. Now, to be sure, in the brilliant forenoon sun, rocks the size of a human head kept flying down the snowy cliff, but in the early morning hours we would advance rapidly and without risk.

After this stocktaking the weather turned bad. The five meagre prayer flags that Ang Dorje had fastened with string between the two tents fluttered uneasily in the wind. Otherwise for days we heard nothing but the storm wind against the canvas of the tents, and from time to time the thundering of an avalanche.

What must it have been like when the Sherpas were searching for this crossing and their families were tied down for weeks here? They had survived storms at this altitude in their dark yak-hair tents, with dried dung as fuel and covers made of sheepskin. How unfit we were when it came to survival! In spite of such modern equipment as gas stoves, Goretex tents and down sleeping bags, we feared mortally succumbing to the tempest.

How quickly, in spite of it all, one grew accustomed to the tent from the inside and the bad weather outside! For three whole nights and three whole days, the storm tore away at the canvas coverings.

Then the weather appeared to improve. The backpacks were loaded. I slept restlessly; we could not afford to oversleep.

The ascent to the summit of Cho Oyu. At the bottom left, the base camp. Between the base camp and the summit there is a difference of more than 3000 metres in altitude.

Tea was brewed at three in the morning. We were ready to go shortly after four o'clock; a starlit heaven above, a handwidth of snow on the hard névé foundation. We were in high spirits.

We walked for about an hour in the glow of our flashlights. By the time it was light we were already high up the southwest slope of Cho Oyu. Below us lay the Tibetan high plateau. The glacier that flowed in the direction of Tingri was huge. Since we didn't know the route, our advance was like the solving of a series of mysteries. Curiosity, for all the weariness, urged us on behind every snow-covered ridge, beyond every towering rock. Were there obstacles that could not be overcome? How far was it to the top? Would we make it to that first bivouac underneath projecting ice in the middle of the concave wall?

A measuring rod for endlessness has yet to be discovered.

Around noon of the second day of climbing we took a break on a level ridge. Michl was the first one to get up. With the unpredictable boldness peculiar to the crazed, he now took the lead. He climbed with an air of certainty, went around a towering rock to the right and came triumphantly to a halt on a rise like a visionary. The trek went on.

The night passed slowly. Dressing and starting off in the morning became an act of pure self-mastery. Only Hans radiated self-confidence. We packed everything into our backpacks, bundled the tents, still moist with the night, on top of them and put on the rope.

We climbed up a difficult wall of ice that blocked the view to the summit. Securing myself, I repeatedly looked down to the greyish-green glacier floors. I wondered how the Sherpas of long ago viewed this mountain. As a threat? As protection? As something incomprehensible?

On the summit of Cho Oyu (8201 m). Hans Kammerlander, Michl Dacher and Reinhold Messner climbed the mountain in alpine style. They stood on the highest point on 5 May 1983.

At a height of 7100 metsres we bivouacked for the last time. The horizon was now more distant; there was more sky than snow to see. Not one among the three of us could hide his impatience. In spite of our fatigue, we would have very much liked to have kept on going that very night; perhaps only in order that we could return. The growing uncertainty was genuinely hard to bear.

It didn't come down to actually being on the top, actually arriving. To be on the move without a yesterday and without a tomorrow; that was the trick.

The final night passed slowly. We tossed and turned. It was only when we left the small tent the next morning that our limbs and lungs recovered. Unexpected energy flowed through us in the knowledge that we were heading to the top, to the turnabout point. We went on hour after hour. Pig-headed. Uphill. Once we reached the large flat stretch of snow, we long had the feeling of being at the very top, but we were still ascending. Finally we were standing on one last snowdrift.
We looked at one another with looks I'd seen on the feeble-minded. We were at the top!

Tingri and neighbouring villages at the foot of Cho Oyu to the north. The yeti between the mountain peaks in the middle of the picture reveals the Sherpas' notion of how the snowman looks. The legend surrounding the yeti may have arisen during their migration.

Fog engulfed us. To the north I could see patches of the Tibetan high plateau. The distance to the pastel-coloured plain was impossible to judge. To the south the view descended abruptly over chains of mountains, down to where the ancient forests gave off steam. The Sherpas and the Tibetans call the Himalaya the 'Land of Snow', presumably because they have always seen it from below. I would like to call the Himalaya the land of visions; sky, clouds, fire, water and earth here enter into an uncommon relationship with one another.

Down below, squeezed on to a brown mountain ridge, lay Tingri, a dirty Tibetan village. There the migration of the Sherpas had been interrupted, before they found their way further over the Nangpa La. Some of them had visited the Lamaist monastery of Rongbuk at the northern foot of Chomolungma; others went to Rongshar to the west of Tseringma. Gauri Shankar, also called Tseringma, was the holiest of all mountains for the Sherpas; the Good Mother of Long Life. This peak may have been what floated in their minds as the goal on their long trek from Kham to Solu Khumbu. Which mountain was it, though, that pointed out the way for them? As prominent as Gauri Shankar appears from the south, it was invisible from the north, from the Tibetan high plateau. It lay hidden behind other peaks.

Gokyo Lake in the valley of the same name, surrounded by Himalayan mountains. To the right, Cho Oyu, which appears to touch the sky. To the right of the lake, Gokyo pasture lands.

In the first half of the sixteenth century the children and the emigrants from Kham, and their children after them, approached the mountain on which we were now standing, Cho Oyu. Did the Sherpas confuse it with Tseringma? Did later groups in search of the sacred maternal mountain fall prey to the same mistake? The movements of peoples from Kham to Solu Khumbu extended over a period of centuries, and those in search of land always set their sights on Cho Oyu. For hundreds of kilometres they had the white, gleaming névé surface, the calotte of Cho Oyu's peak, in front of them, as if it were showing them the way.

I looked south. Through a hole in the clouds I saw Gokyo Lake. Water and ice appeared green, like virgin grass, mineral green, as if the colours of heaven and earth had combined in it. Towards the middle of the lake I recognised the clear turquoise green of an iris, an eye of the Goddess of Turquoise.

A view from Thame Valley towards Kusum Kangri (at the extreme right). All of these pictures were painted on canvas. Size: 60 x 40 centimetres.

That same day we descended to the last bivouac, and on the following day to the forward base camp on the Nangpa La. It was night when we arrived. We lay down to sleep without talking about what we had experienced.

The solitude up above, the days of wordless company with one another in storm and under stress, had reconciled us. What was experienced was not for any one individual, not for one person apart from the next. We didn't need to talk.

The following day we slowly began the trek back to the valley.

I sat alone one quiet evening in May at the edge of a small lake. After eight hours of walking and after the hard days on Cho Oyu, I set myself down in order to give wings to my thoughts. It was fairly cool. An icy wind rippled the surface of the water. I had been sitting for a long while on a rock, with my jacket as a cushion, when the yak drivers came by. Their whistling and the rhythmic clang of the bells harmonised so well with my mood that I forgot the success on the peak.

The next day, on the way from Thame to Namche Bazaar, the white, triple-capped Kusum Kangri rose far out in the valley. Its peak projected ghostlike from the fog, as if it were a guide. It, too, was a divine mountain for the Sherpas.

In Namche Bazaar we put up in the same hotel as on the way up. The shabbiness of the place I now found charming.

When a pair of locals congratulated me the next morning on our success on Cho Oyu, they kept looking in the direction of the mountain, without being able to see it. It was as if they wanted to point out the direction they had once come from.

Cho Oyu was for the Sherpas the guide to the legendary territory of the three sisters, Ama Dablam, Chomolungma and the previously mentioned Tseringma, which is still revered by all Central Asiatic peoples as the holiest of mountains. Now it was the beacon into the past, back to where they had started out. These Sherpas worried as little about the king of Nepal as they had about the power of the Dalai Lama in their original homeland of Kham. Little by little an agreement was reached between the government of Nepal and the Sherpas, who enjoyed an autonomy of sorts. The Sherpa people have preserved a great deal of freedom for themselves.

Gokyo Lake and (at the extreme right) Cho Oyu. When no tourists and mountain climbers are around, Khumbu is as peaceful as it was centuries ago.

On our flight to Kathmandu on May 15 in a Twin Otter I saw Cho Oyu for the last time. The Goddess of Turquoise was far away. Her face became hidden in the chain of the Himalaya, and so too her secret was hidden. The influence of this mountain deity extended as far as the peak could be seen by human eye.

During these minutes between one world and the other, I knew that this earth can only be saved if man takes his measure from Nature, the deity, if he takes his bearings from the powers that Sherpas have oriented themselves towards for centuries.

They held commerce with what was needed, though neither with industrial goods nor with messages from heaven. Nor was 'doing good' a calling in the Himalaya. Each went his own way; the trees, the soil, the mountains were the standard for all men.

In our enslavement to the present utilitarian delusions emanating from the West, we have plundered Nature, expelled the gods, decoded the world. Nothing the while would be of greater utility than to know where we are heading. Will we find the way forward without something to go by?

A Bibliography of the Most Important Publications about the Sherpas

Axelsen, H. G.: The Sherpas of the Solu District. A preliminary Report on Ethnological Field Research in the Solu District of N. E. Nepal, Copenhagen, 1977.

Baumgartner, R.: Trekking and Entwicklung im Himalaya. Die Rolwaling Sherpa in Ost-Nepal im Dilemma zwischen Hourismus ad Tradition. Diessenhofen (C. H.), Ruegger, 1981.

Bista, D. B.: People of Nepal, Kathmandu, Ratna Pustak Bhandar, 1967; Nachdruck 1972, 1976, 1980.

Bourdillon, J.: Visit to the Sherpas, London, Collins, 1956.

Bourdillon, J. & V. Coverley-Price: The Sherpas of Nepal, Oxford University Press, 1958.

Doig, D.: Sherpaland in: National Geographic Magazine (Washington), Oct. 1966.

Fantin, M.: I monastery della regione del Khumbu, in: L'Universo, (Florenz), 1971.

Fantin, M.: Mani Rimdu, Bologna, 1976 (Englische Ubersetzung): Mani Rimdu, Nepal. The Buddhist Dance Drama of Tengboche, New Delhi, English Bookstore, 1980.

Funke, F. W.: Religioses Leben der Sherpa in: Khumbu Himal, Band IX, Innsbruck/Munchen, Wagner, 1969.

Funke, F, W.: Die Sherpa und ihre Nachbarolker im Himalaya, Frankfurt, W. Kruger, 1978.

Furer-Haimendorf, C. von: The Sherpas of Nepal, Buddhist Highlanders, London, Murray, 1964; Nachdruck 1972.

Hagen, T. et al.: Mount Everedst, Oxford University Press, 1963.

Hagen, T.: Nepal, Bern, Kummerly and Frey, 1971 (Text in Englisch).

Hagen, N.: In highest Nepal. Our Life among the Sherpa, Allen and Unwin, 1957.

Hillary, E.: We build a School for Sherpa Children, in: National Geographic Magazine (Washington), Oct. 1962.

Jerstad, L. G.: Mani-Rimdu. Sherpa Dance Drama. Seattle, University of Washington Press, 1969.

MacDonald, A. W.: Creative Dismemberment among the Tamang and the Sherpas of Nepal, in: Tibetan Studies in Honour of H. Richardson (ed. M. Aris and Oppitz, M.: Geschichte und Sozialordnung der Sherpa, in: Khumbu Himal, Band VIII, Innsbruck/Munchen, Wagner, 1968.

Oppitz, M.: Myths and Facts: Reconsidering some Data concerning the Clan History of the Sherpa, in: Contributions to the Anthropology of Nepal (ed. C. von furer-Haimendori), University of London; Warminster, Aris & Phillips, 1974.

Ortner. S. B.: Sherpa Purity, in: American Anthropologist, Band 75, 1973.

Ortner, S. B.: Sherpas through their Rituals, Cambridge University Press, 1978.

Paul. R.: Some Observations on Sherpa Schamanism, in: Spirit Possession in the Nepal Himalayas (ed.) J. T. Hitchcok & R. L. Jones): Warminster, Aris and Phillips, 1976.

Rudolph, F. Himalaya-tigers. Der Kampf um das Dach der Welt, Berlin, Sportverlag, 1956.

Sacherer, J. M.: Sherpas of the rolwaling Valley. Human Adaptation to harsh Mountain Environment, in: Objects et Mondes (Paris), Band XIV/4, 1974.

Schmidt-Thome, M. & T. T. Thingo: Materielle Kultur and Kunst der Sherpa, in: Khumbu Himal, Band III, Innsbruck/Munchen, Wagner, 1975.

Sen, D. & P. M. Mackenzie: Himalaya. I monastery dei Lama (L'Universo dello Spirito), Milano, Mondadori, 1982.

Sestini, V. & E. Somigli: Aspetti architettonici degli insediamenti Sherpa nella Valle di Khumbu, in: Lhotse 75, Bologna, Tamari, 1977.

Sestini, V. & E. Somigli: Sherpa Architecture, Paris, Unesco, 1978.

Styles, F. S.: Sherpa Adventure, New York, 1960.

Teschk, G. C.: Anthropologie des Sherpas, in: Khumbu Himal, Band XI, Innsbruck/Munchen, Wagner, 1977.

Die Reihe Khumbu Himal, von der bisher 14 Bande erschienen sind, bietet ein auberst reiches Register aller Aspekte des Verbreitungsgebietes der Sherpas; sie wird herausgegeben vom Universitatsverlag Wagner (Innsbruck and Munchen), und vom Springer Verlag in Berlin unter der Leitung von Walter Hellmich. Die Reihe wurde im jahre 1964 begonnen. Siehe dazu die Ubersicht aller Titel in: Yakushi, Yoshimi: Catalogue of Himalayan Literature, Tokio, Hakushusha, 1984.

Allgemeine Literatur uber Tibet:

Getty, A.: the Gods of Northern Buddhism, Oxford, 1928; Nachdruck Tokyo, Tuttle, 1963.

Lindegger, P.: Onomasticon Tibetanum, Rikon, Tibet-Institut 1976.

Shakabpa, tsepon W. D.: Tibet, a Political History, Yale University Press, 1967.

Snellgrove, D.: Buddhist Himalaya, Oxford, Cassirer, 1957.

Snellgrove, D. & H. Richardson: A Cultural History of Tibet, London, Weidenfeld and Nicolson, 1968; Nachdruck Boulder (Colorado), Pranja Press 1980 (mit Bibliographie).

Stein, R. A.: La civilization Tibetaine, Paris 1962.

Tucci, G.: Tibet, Paese delle Nevi, Novara, De Agostini, 1968.

Verschiedene Autoren: Tibet, Milano, Touring Club Italiano, 1981.

Verschiedene Autoren: The Potala Palace of Tibet. Shanghai People's Art Publishing House, Hongkong, Joint Publishing Co. 1982.

MORE TITLES ON MOUNTAINEERING AND TREKKING FROM PILGRIMS PUBLISHING

- **Among the Himalayas** .... *L A Waddel*
- **Annapurna South Face** .... *Chris Bonington*
- **Attack on Everest** .... *Hugh Ruttledge*
- **Climbing the Fish Tail** .... *Wilfred Noyce*
- **Everest:** From the first attempt to the final victory. .... *Micheline Morin*
- **Everest the Challenge** .... *Sir Francis Younghusband*
- **Everest: the Hard Way (The adventure story of the Decade)** .... *Chris Bonington*
- **First Over Everest:** The Huston-Mount Everest Expedition 1933
  .... *P F M Fellowes, L V Stewart Blacker, P T Etherton & others*
- **Himalayan Adventure Trekking Gear:** A Checklist for Women .... *Joyce A Tapper*
- **Lost in the Himalayas** .... *James Scott & Joanne Robertson*
- **Mansalu: A Trekker's Guide** .... *Kev Reynolds*
- **Man of Everest** .... *James Ramsey Ullman*
- **Mount Everest 1938** .... *H W Tilman*
- **Mount Everest :** The Reconnaissance 1921 .... *C K Howard-Bury*
- **Mustang: A Trekking Guide** .... *Bob Gibbons and Sian Prichard-Jones*

- **Mustang: Un Guide de Trekking** .... *Bob Gibbons and Sian Prichard-Jones*
- **Nepal Die Far Western Region:**
  Reisecompanion für Abenteurer, Trekker und Bergsteiger .... *M Lindenfelser*
- **Nepal Himalaya** .... *H W Tilman*
- **Nepal the Far Western Region:**
  A Travelling Companion for Travellers, Trekkers and Climbers .... *M Lindenfelser*
- **Peaks and Lamas** .... *Marco Pallis*
- **Round Kangchenjunga** .... *Douglas W Freshfield*
- **The Assault on Mount Everest 1922** .... *C G Bruce*
- **The Epic of Mount Everest** .... *Sir Francis Younghusband*
- **The Fight for Everest 1924** .... *E F Norton*
- **The High Altitude Medicine Handbook** .... *A J Pollard & D R Murdoch*
- **The Himalayas** (An illustrated summary of the World's Highest Mountain Ranges)
  .... *Edited by David Mordecai*
- **The Kangchenjunga Adventure** .... *F S Smythe*
- **The Land of the Sherpas** .... *Ella Maillart*

www.pilgrimsbooks.com

For catalog and more information, mail or fax to:

PILGRIMS BOOK HOUSE
Mail Order, P.O.Box 3872, Kathmandu, Nepal
Tel: 977-1-4700919 Fax: 977-1-4700943
E-mail: mailorder@pilgrims.wlink.com.np